D0564626

NEEDLEWORK DESIGNS FOR MINIATURE PROJECTS

64 Charts for Counted Cross-Stitch and Needlepoint

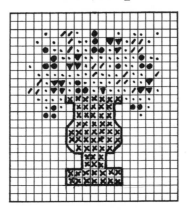

Eileen Folk

Dover Publications, Inc.
New York

To John Andrew
and Elizabeth Anne with love
and to RML,
who knows that neatness counts.

Copyright © 1984 by Eileen Folk.
All rights reserved under Pan American and International Copyright Conventions.

Published in Canada by General Publishing Company, Ltd., 30 Lesmill Road, Don Mills, Toronto, Ontario.
Published in the United Kingdom by Constable and Company, Ltd.

Edited by Linda Macho.

Needlework Designs for Miniature Projects is a new work, first published by Dover Publications, Inc., in 1984.

Manufactured in the United States of America
Dover Publications, Inc., 31 East 2nd Street, Mineola, N.Y. 11501

Library of Congress Cataloging in Publication Data

Folk, Eileen.
  Needlework designs for miniature projects.

  1. Cross-stitch—Patterns. 2. Canvas embroidery—Patterns. 3. Miniature craft.   I. Title.
TT778.C76F65   1984   746.44   83-20535
ISBN 0-486-24660-4

CONTENTS

INTRODUCTION

Mention miniatures and the uninitiated think of a delightful if unrealistic hobby, limited to the decoration of dollhouses. What they don't realize is that while collecting miniatures may have begun that way, this hobby has proven to be the catalyst in starting a chain reaction of excitement, learning, creativity and innovation. True miniature enthusiasts have found themselves inadvertently learning crafts and needlework they would never have considered trying in full scale. For instance, miniature lovers have taken up woodworking so they could build their own dollhouses and furniture. They have begun knitting and crocheting so they could fashion their own afghans, doilies, tablecloths and other accessories. They've started sewing to make quilts, pillows, draperies and many other decorative items. They have learned how to sculpt so they could fashion flowers, fruits, cakes, meats and other miniature necessities of life.

Now with this volume, miniature enthusiasts can add two other types of needlework to their repertoire: counted cross-stitch and needlepoint. This book contains 64 charted designs that encompass everything a home decorator would need to enhance any room with a minimum of effort and a maximum of style. Designed for both beginners and more experienced needleworkers, all the projects should be tackled in the same way—one stitch at a time—with care and attention to detail.

Both counted cross-stitch and needlepoint can be worked from charts. Each square on the charts is the equivalent of one stitch worked in either technique. All of the colors are suggestions. Unless you are designing a room completely from scratch, use a color scheme that will coordinate with pieces you already have. If you do change the color scheme, try to replace the dark colors with darks and light colors with lights to preserve the concept of the design. Specific instructions and color keys are given where necessary with each design. Finishing instructions and other suggestions precede each separate type of project.

Keep in mind that the finished piece of needlework will not be the same size as the charted design unless you happen to be working on fabric (or canvas) that has the same number of threads-per-inch as the chart has squares-per-inch. To determine how large a finished design will be, divide the number of stitches in the design by the thread-count or mesh-count of the fabric or canvas. For example, if a design that is 44 stitches wide by 66 stitches deep is worked on a 22-count Hardanger cloth, the worked design will measure 2″ × 3″. The same design worked on 18-mesh needlepoint canvas would measure approximately 2½″ × 3⅝″. Therefore, in all cases, the designs worked in counted cross-stitch will end up being smaller than their needlepoint counterparts. Many of the more delicate designs such as the samplers, screens and bellpulls may tend to look bulky if worked in needlepoint. Other designs such as the quilts, curtains and bedspreads should *only* be worked in counted cross-stitch. Where there may be a problem with a certain technique, instructions will be given in the introductory paragraph preceding the section.

Room Suggestions

If you already own a furnished dollhouse, I hope that you will use these designs to enhance your furnishings and enliven rooms that may need a new decorative element. If you are decorating an unfurnished dollhouse or creating a miniature vignette, I would like to suggest some combinations that will assist you in your endeavors. Following are five different room ideas based on the designs in this book. You can see some of these rooms in full color on the covers of this book.

ORIENTAL DINING ROOM
Shown in color on the front cover.

Instructions for Counted Cross-Stitch

Many of these designs were created for counted cross-stitch; one of the great advantages to this craft is that the supplies and equipment required are minimal and inexpensive. You will need:

1. A small blunt tapestry needle, #24 or #26.

2. Evenweave fabric. To achieve the correct scale for miniatures, use Hardanger cloth, which has 22 threads-per-inch and is available in cotton or linen.

3. Embroidery thread. This should be six-strand mercerized cotton floss (DMC, Coats and Clark, Lily, Anchor, etc.). Use only one strand of floss to embroider miniature projects unless otherwise directed. One skein of each color given in the color key is needed; usually, however, you will not use up an entire skein of floss, so one skein can be used to embroider several projects.

4. Embroidery hoop. Use a plastic or wooden 4", 5" or 6" round or oval hoop with a screw-type tension adjuster.

5. A pair of sharp embroidery scissors is absolutely essential.

Prepare the fabric by whipping, hemming or zigzagging on the sewing machine to prevent raveling at the edges. Next, locate the exact center of the design you have chosen, so that you can then center the design on the piece of fabric. Then, find the center of the fabric by folding it in half both vertically and horizontally. The center stitch of the design should fall where the creases in the fabric meet.

It's usually not very convenient to begin work with the center stitch itself. As a rule it's better to start at the top of a design, working horizontal rows of a single color, left to right. This technique permits you to go from an unoccupied space to an occupied space (from an empty hole to a filled one), which makes ruffling the floss less likely. To find out where the top of the design should be placed, count squares up from the center of the design, and then count off the corresponding number of holes up from the center of the fabric.

Next, place the section of the fabric to be worked tautly in the hoop; the tighter the better, for tension makes it easier to push the needle through the holes without piercing the fabric. As you work, use the screw adjuster to tighten as necessary. Keep the screw at the top and out of your way.

Counted cross-stitch is very simple. When beginning, fasten thread with a waste knot by holding a bit of thread on the underside of the work and anchoring it with the first few stitches (*diagram 1*). To stitch, push the threaded needle up through a hole in the fabric and cross over the thread intersection (or square) diagonally, left to right (*diagram 2*). This is half the stitch. Now cross back, right to left, making an

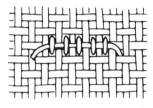

DIAGRAM 1
Reverse side of work

DIAGRAM 2

X (*diagram 3*). Do all the stitches in the same color in the same row, working left to right and slanting from bottom left to upper right (*diagram 3*). Then cross back, completing the X's (*diagram 4*). Some cross-stitchers prefer to cross each stitch as they come to it; this is fine, but be sure the slant is always in the correct direction. Of course, isolated stitches must be crossed as you work them. Vertical stitches are

DIAGRAM 3

DIAGRAM 4

crossed as shown in *diagram 5*. Holes are used more than once; all stitches "hold hands" unless a space is indicated. The work is always held upright, never turned as for some needlepoint stitches.

DIAGRAM 5

When carrying a color from one area to another, wiggle your needle under existing stitches on the underside. Do not carry a color across an open expanse of fabric for more than a few stitches, as the thread will be visible from the front. Remember, in counted cross-stitch you do not work the background.

To end a color, weave in and out of the underside of stitches, perhaps making a scallop stitch or two for extra security (*diagram 6*). Whenever possible, end in the direction in which you are traveling, jumping up a row if necessary (*diagram 7*). This prevents holes

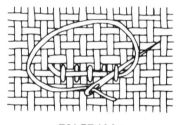

DIAGRAM 6
Reverse side of work

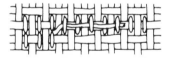

DIAGRAM 7
Reverse side of work

caused by work being pulled in two directions. Do not make knots; knots make bumps. Cut off the ends of the threads; do not leave any tails because they'll show through when the work is mounted.

Another stitch used in counted cross-stitch is the back-stitch. This is worked from hole to hole and may be vertical, horizontal or slanted (*diagram 8*).

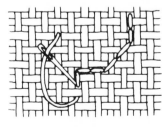

DIAGRAM 8

For a special effect, French knots, straight stitch or lazy daisy stitch may be recommended. These stitches can be worked in the normal fashion (*diagram 9*).

After you have completed your embroidery, wash it in cool or lukewarm water with a mild soap. Rinse well. Do not wring. Roll in a towel to remove excess moisture. Immediately iron on a padded surface with the embroidery face down. Be sure the embroidery is completely dry before attempting to mount it.

French Knot   *Straight Stitch*   *Lazy Daisy Stitch*

DIAGRAM 9

Instructions for Needlepoint

Charted designs can also be used for needlepoint. The designs can be worked directly onto needlepoint canvas by counting off the correct number of warp and weft squares shown on the chart, each square representing one stitch to be taken on the canvas. If you prefer to put some guidelines on the canvas, make certain that your marking medium is waterproof. Use either nonsoluble inks, acrylic paints thinned appropriately with water so as not to clog the holes in the canvas, or oil paints mixed with benzine or turpentine. Felt-tipped pens are very handy, but check the labels carefully because not all felt markers are waterproof. It is a good idea to experiment with any writing materials on a piece of scrap canvas to make certain that all material is waterproof. There is nothing worse than having a bit of ink run onto the needlepoint as you are blocking it.

There are two distinct types of needlepoint canvas: single-mesh and double-mesh. Double-mesh is woven with two horizontal and two vertical threads forming each mesh, whereas single-mesh is woven with one vertical and one horizontal thread forming each mesh. Double-mesh is a very stable canvas on which the threads will stay securely in place as you work. Single-mesh canvas, which is more widely used, is a little easier on the eyes because the spaces are slightly larger. To achieve the correct miniature scale of 1″ = 1′, use size 18 needlepoint canvas. A single ply of wool or six strands of embroidery floss will adequately cover the canvas. Use a tapestry needle with a rounded, blunt tip and an elongated eye; the needle should clear the hole in the canvas without spreading the threads.

For most of the designs in this book, the best results will be achieved if the continental stitch is used to work details in the designs and the basketweave stitch is used to fill in the background after the details have been completed. The exceptions are the upholstery designs; these are worked in bargello stitch following the charts.

CONTINENTAL STITCH (*diagram 10*). Start this design at the upper right-hand corner and work from right to left. The needle is slanted and always brought out a mesh ahead. The resulting stitch is actually a half-

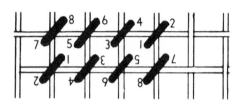

DIAGRAM 10

cross stitch on top and a slanting stitch on the back. When the row is finished, turn the canvas around and work the return row, still stitching from right to left.

BASKETWEAVE STITCH (*diagram 11*). Start in the upper right-hand corner of the area with four continental stitches, two worked horizontally across the top and two placed directly below the first stitch. Then work diagonal rows, the first slanting up and across the canvas from right to left and the next down and across from left to right. Each new row is one stitch longer. As you go down the canvas (left to right), the needle is held in a vertical position; as you move in the opposite direction, the needle is horizontal. The rows should interlock, creating a basketweave pattern on the reverse. If this is not done properly, a faint ridge will show where the pattern was interrupted. Always stop working in the middle of a row, rather than at the end, so that you will know in which direction you were working.

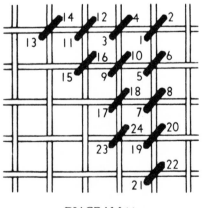

DIAGRAM 11

Bind all the raw edges of needlepoint canvas with masking tape, double-fold bias tape or even adhesive tape. There are no set rules on where to begin a design. Generally it is easier to begin close to the center and work outward toward the edges of the canvas, working the backgrounds or borders last. To avoid fraying the yarn, work with strands not longer than 18".

When you have finished your needlepoint, it should be blocked. No matter how straight you have kept your work, blocking will give it a professional look.

Any hard, flat surface that you do not mind marring with nail holes and one that will not be warped by wet needlepoint can serve as a blocking board. A piece of plywood, an old drawing board or an old-fashioned doily blocker are ideal.

Moisten a Turkish towel in cold water and roll the needlepoint in the towel. Leaving the needlepoint in the towel overnight will insure that both the canvas and the yarn are thoroughly and evenly dampened. Do not saturate the needlepoint! Never hold the needlepoint under the faucet as that much water is not necessary.

Mark the desired outline on the blocking board, making sure that the corners are straight. Lay the needlepoint on the blocking board, and tack the canvas with thumbtacks spaced about ½" to ¾" apart. It will probably take a good deal of pulling and tugging to get the needlepoint straight, but do not be afraid of this stress. Leave the canvas on the blocking board until thoroughly dry. Never put an iron on your needlepoint. You cannot successfully block with a steam iron because the needlepoint must dry in the straightened position.

METRIC CONVERSION CHART

CONVERTING INCHES TO CENTIMETERS AND YARDS TO METERS

mm — millimeters   cm — centimeters   m — meters

INCHES INTO MILLIMETERS AND CENTIMETERS
(Slightly rounded off for convenience)

inches	mm		cm	inches	cm	inches	cm	inches	cm
1/8	3mm			5	12.5	21	53.5	38	96.5
1/4	6mm			5½	14	22	56	39	99
3/8	10mm	or	1cm	6	15	23	58.5	40	101.5
1/2	13mm	or	1.3cm	7	18	24	61	41	104
5/8	15mm	or	1.5cm	8	20.5	25	63.5	42	106.5
3/4	20mm	or	2cm	9	23	26	66	43	109
7/8	22mm	or	2.2cm	10	25.5	27	68.5	44	112
1	25mm	or	2.5cm	11	28	28	71	45	114.5
1¼	32mm	or	3.2cm	12	30.5	29	73.5	46	117
1½	38mm	or	3.8cm	13	33	30	76	47	119.5
1¾	45mm	or	4.5cm	14	35.5	31	79	48	122
2	50mm	or	5cm	15	38	32	81.5	49	124.5
2½	65mm	or	6.5cm	16	40.5	33	84	50	127
3	75mm	or	7.5cm	17	43	34	86.5		
3½	90mm	or	9cm	18	46	35	89		
4	100mm	or	10cm	19	48.5	36	91.5		
4½	115mm	or	11.5cm	20	51	37	94		

YARDS TO METERS
(Slightly rounded off for convenience)

yards	meters	yards	meters	yards	meters	yards	meters	yards	meters
1/8	0.15	2⅛	1.95	4⅛	3.80	6⅛	5.60	8⅛	7.45
1/4	0.25	2¼	2.10	4¼	3.90	6¼	5.75	8¼	7.55
3/8	0.35	2⅜	2.20	4⅜	4.00	6⅜	5.85	8⅜	7.70
1/2	0.50	2½	2.30	4½	4.15	6½	5.95	8½	7.80
5/8	0.60	2⅝	2.40	4⅝	4.25	6⅝	6.10	8⅝	7.90
3/4	0.70	2¾	2.55	4¾	4.35	6¾	6.20	8¾	8.00
7/8	0.80	2⅞	2.65	4⅞	4.50	6⅞	6.30	8⅞	8.15
1	0.95	3	2.75	5	4.60	7	6.40	9	8.25
1⅛	1.05	3⅛	2.90	5⅛	4.70	7⅛	6.55	9⅛	8.35
1¼	1.15	3¼	3.00	5¼	4.80	7¼	6.65	9¼	8.50
1⅜	1.30	3⅜	3.10	5⅜	4.95	7⅜	6.75	9⅜	8.60
1½	1.40	3½	3.20	5½	5.05	7½	6.90	9½	8.70
1⅝	1.50	3⅝	3.35	5⅝	5.15	7⅝	7.00	9⅝	8.80
1¾	1.60	3¾	3.45	5¾	5.30	7¾	7.10	9¾	8.95
1⅞	1.75	3⅞	3.55	5⅞	5.40	7⅞	7.20	9⅞	9.05
2	1.85	4	3.70	6	5.50	8	7.35	10	9.15

AVAILABLE FABRIC WIDTHS

25"	65cm	50"	127cm
27"	70cm	54"/56"	140cm
35"/36"	90cm	58"/60"	150cm
39"	100cm	68"/70"	175cm
44"/45"	115cm	72"	180cm
48"	122cm		

AVAILABLE ZIPPER LENGTHS

4"	10cm	10"	25cm	22"	55cm
5"	12cm	12"	30cm	24"	60cm
6"	15cm	14"	35cm	26"	65cm
7"	18cm	16"	40cm	28"	70cm
8"	20cm	18"	45cm	30"	75cm
9"	22cm	20"	50cm		

RUGS

A rug will add warmth and charm to any miniature setting, and it is an excellent place to begin planning your decorating scheme—both color- and style-wise. Featured here are five rugs sure to fit in with many different decorating styles. Work each rug on size 18 needlepoint canvas, working the design in continental stitch and the background in basketweave stitch. Use a single ply of Persian wool or six strands of embroidery floss. Refer to pages 8–9 for complete needlepoint instructions.

Fringing a Rug: Trim away excess canvas, leaving three rows of unworked mesh around the edge of the design. Apply diluted glue sparingly to the edges and allow to dry thoroughly; this will prevent the canvas from fraying. Work the fringe over the three rows of unworked canvas in each mesh all around following *Diagram 12*. Use a small latch hook* and 1¼–1½"

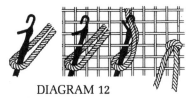

DIAGRAM 12

length of yarn. Insert latch hook from bottom to top through innermost mesh of canvas and position length of yarn across hook. Draw yarn through mesh leaving tails on top of canvas. Insert tails through loop. Draw loop tight. Trim edges of fringe evenly when finished.

Binding a Rug: Trim away excess canvas, leaving two rows of unworked mesh around the straight edges of the design. If the rug is curved or circular, leave three rows around the edge to prevent fraying. Apply glue same as when fringing a rug. Work the binding over the two or three rows of unworked canvas in each mesh all around following *Diagram 13*; use two

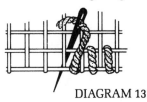

DIAGRAM 13

strands of wool in needle for a raised effect. Do not make knots; end by running excess yarn beneath stitches on back of work.

Lining a Rug: To give a professional, finished appearance to your miniature rug, line the back with lightweight fabric in a matching color. Cut the fabric to the same size as the finished rug (minus fringe); press the raw edges of the fabric ⅛–¼" to the wrong side, depending upon how the edge is finished, and sew to the wrong side of the rug with matching sewing thread and a needle; make tiny overcast stitches.

Hooked Rug: The appearance of a hooked rug can be simulated by stitching the entire design on the canvas using French knots. This is a good way to achieve an old-fashioned or antique appearance.

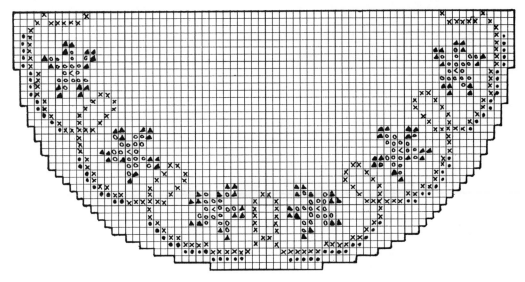

FLORAL HEARTH RUG
(inside front cover)

Color Key

☐	white	⊡	light pink	☒	light green
◁	yellow	▲	medium pink	⊙	medium green

Bind the edges of the rug with white.

*There is a very tiny latch hook sold at the sewing notions counter. Its actual purpose is to draw pulled threads on machine knits to the wrong side of the fabric. While the product makes no mention of other uses, it is a good piece of equipment for miniature enthusiasts to know about. Use it in exactly the same manner as a large latch hook.

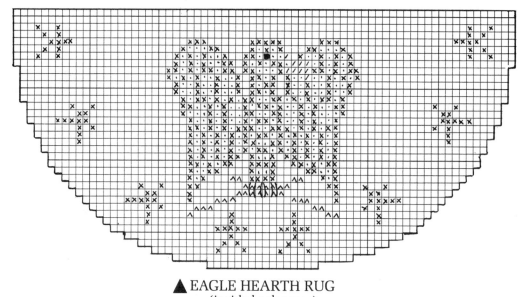

▲EAGLE HEARTH RUG
(inside back cover)

Color Key

☑	white	☒	medium gold
⋀	tan	☐	navy blue
⊡	light gold	◼	black

Work the eagle and olive branches first. Before working the background, straight-stitch the talons (⫷   ⫸) using two strands of pale gold embroidery floss. Bind the edges of the rug with navy blue.

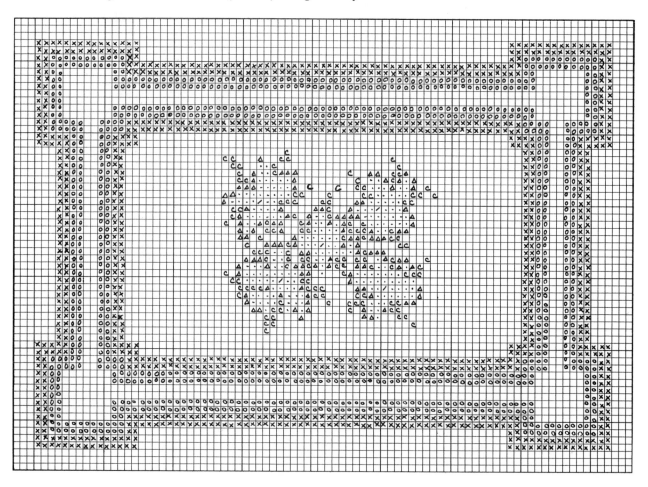

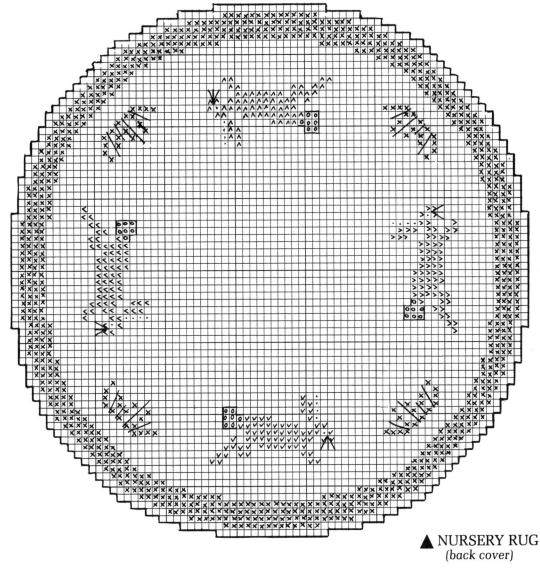

▲ NURSERY RUG
(back cover)

Color Key

☒	green
☑	brown
⊡	dark brown
⊙	white (French knot)

Outline tail and work whiskers in back-stitch using two strands of dark brown floss. Work grass in straight stitch using two strands of dark green floss. Work background in white. Fringe the edges of the rug with white.

◄ FLORAL AREA RUG

Color Key

☐	white
⊡	light yellow
◸	dark yellow
◿	medium blue
⊙	light green
⊡	medium green
☒	dark green

Bind the long edges and fringe the short edges of the rug with white.

upper left

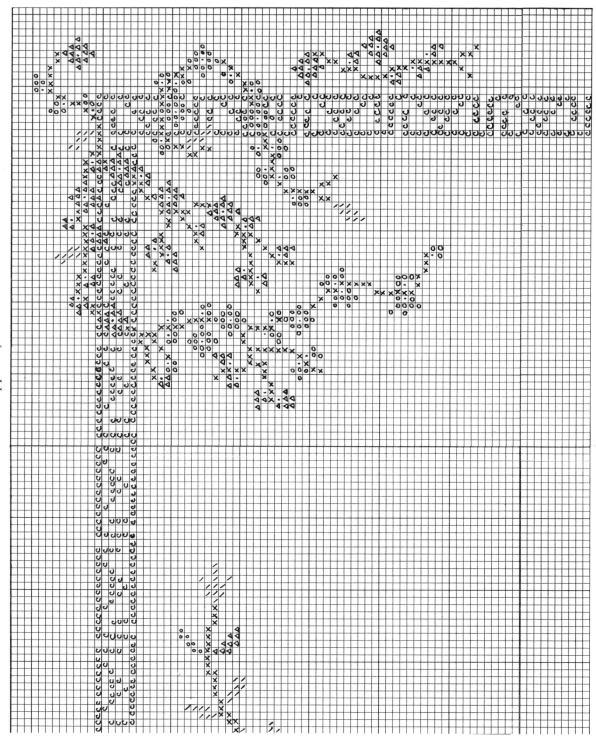

TREE-OF-LIFE CARPET
(front cover)

Color Key

☾	ecru	☐	blue
·	light yellow	◢	medium green
☉	dark yellow	☒	tan
◁	medium pink	▷	dark brown

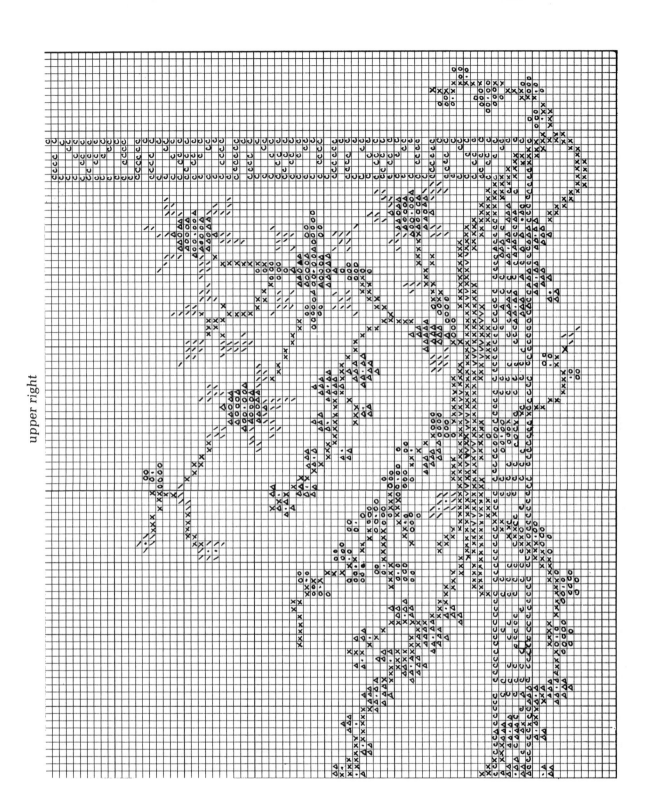

For ease in execution, work the geometric border first, then the design. Work the background last. Traditional rugs of this type can also be worked with ivory or brown backgrounds, depending upon the color scheme of your dollhouse. Bind the long edges of the carpet with the background color; fringe the short edges of the carpet with 1½″ lengths of ecru. Charts for the lower half of the carpet are on pages 16–17.

lower left

TREE-OF-LIFE CARPET
(front cover)

Color Key

⊍	ecru	☐	blue
·	light yellow	◻	medium green
◯	dark yellow	☒	tan
◁	medium pink	▷	dark brown

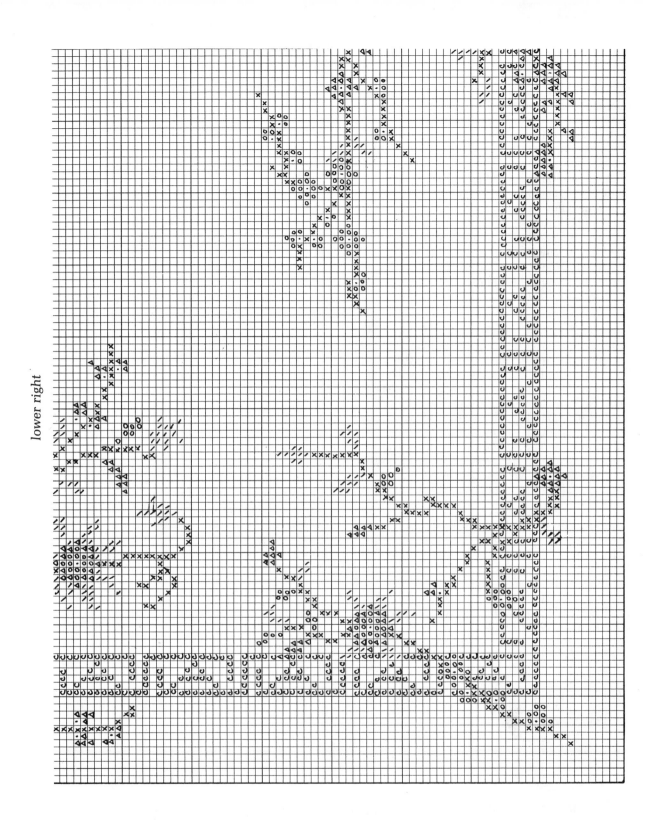

lower right

For ease in execution, work the geometric border first, then the design. Work the background last. Traditional rugs of this type can also be worked with ivory or brown backgrounds, depending upon the color scheme of your dollhouse. Bind the long edges of the carpet with the background color; fringe the short edges of the carpet with 1½" lengths of ecru. Charts for the upper half of the carpet are on pages 14–15.

PILLOWS

Pillows are truly a home decorator's delight—use them as much as you can when decorating your miniature rooms. Pillows will add a bright spot of color to a dark area and can be used effectively to blend several different colors into a harmonious decorating scheme.

I have used Hardanger 22-per-inch counted-thread fabric for all the pillows shown on the covers of this book. The pillow backs may be the same material or a contrasting fabric; also, velvet and satin ribbon work well. For the stuffing, use cotton balls or polyester fiberfill. It's a nice touch to embroider your initials and the date on the back of each pillow. Use two strands of six-strand embroidery floss to embroider each design.

Finishing Square and Rectangular Pillows: Cut the counted-thread fabric ¼″ beyond the edge of the design (indicated by the dark outline around the chart). Cut the backing material or ribbon the same size as the pillow front. With the right sides facing, sew the front to the back on three sides using matching thread and making ¼″ seams. Trim the seams to ⅛″; clip corners diagonally. Turn the pillow to the right side, gently poking out the corners with a crochet hook. Stuff pillow until plump, making sure that the corners are firmly stuffed. Fold the raw edges of the open end ¼″ inside and slip-stitch invisibly to secure.

Finishing Round Pillows: After the design has been worked, use a small lid, a quarter or a compass to draw a circle approximately ½″ larger than the desired size of the finished pillow. Sew approximately ⅛″ outside the desired circle size using small hand-basting stitches. Cut out the circle just beyond the basting stitches. Gently pull the basting thread so the pillow assumes a circular shape. Repeat for the pillow back.

Insert stuffing into each half and slip-stitch together invisibly to secure.

Finishing Oddly Shaped Pillows: Some interesting effects can be achieved when using pillows with a distinctive shape. After the embroidery is complete, cut out the fabric ¼″ beyond the edge of the design (indicated by the dark outline around the chart). Cut a matching piece of fabric for the lining. Carefully sew the pieces together with right sides facing, making a ¼″ seam; leave a ¾″ opening along one edge. When sewing the pieces together, it is important to sew slowly and carefully with very small stitches so as to preserve the contours of the design. After sewing, clip corners diagonally, trim the seam allowance to ⅛″ and clip into the seam allowance to the stitching line at any sharp corners (such as the center "V" of the heart). Also clip any curved edges to the stitching line. Turn to the right side and stuff until plump; stuff carefully to achieve the correct shape. Fold the raw edges at the opening ¼″ inside and slip-stitch invisibly to secure.

Adding Lace: A pillow can be made to look very feminine and/or Victorian by adding lace around the edges. This must be done before the front and back are sewn together. Also, you must use a lace that is compatible in scale with the pillow; use very narrow (⅛–¼″) and finely made lace trim. Ruffled lace trim gives a very frilly effect. Baste the lace by hand to the right side of the pillow front so the raw edges of the pillow and the lace are even. Start at one corner, continuing all around; pleat the lace at the corners to ease. Sew the pillow front to the pillow back, sandwiching the lace in between and being careful not to catch the free edges of the lace in the stitching. Turn to the right side, carefully pulling the lace outward. Sew the opening closed, allowing the lace to extend evenly beyond the edge.

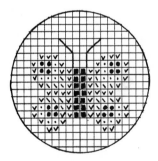

BUTTERFLY PILLOW
(inside front cover)

Color Key

⊡	pink	☑	dark blue
⊙	rose	▣	black
◣	light blue		

Backstitch antennae with one strand of black. Add lace to the edges for a feminine bedroom.

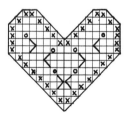

HEART PILLOW
(inside front cover)

Color Key

☒	pink	⊙	red

Backstitch stems with one strand of medium green; backstitch outline of pillow with two strands of red. Add lace to the edges for a romantic touch.

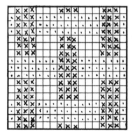

WOVEN PILLOW

Color Key

⊡	yellow	☒	green

This design will look wonderful in many different color combinations. It is an excellent way to combine diverse colors into a coordinated color scheme.

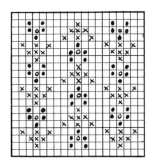

FLOWERS-IN-ROWS PILLOW
(inside front cover)

Color Key

▢	yellow	◉	rose
☒	green		

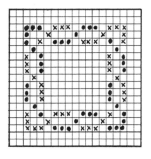

INTERTWINED PILLOW
(inside back cover)

Color Key

☒	medium blue	◉	dark blue

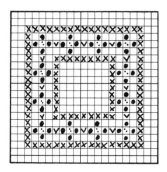

FLOWERS-IN-A-SQUARE PILLOW

Color Key

◉	dark yellow	⊡	medium blue
☑	medium green	☒	dark green

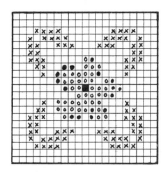

FLORAL PILLOW
(inside front cover)

Color Key

◼	yellow	◉	rose
▢	pink	☒	green

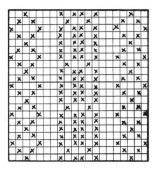

ARAN PILLOW
(inside back cover)

Color Key

☒	medium blue

This design is very effective when stitched white-on-white. Leave no unworked margins around the edges for the true Aran effect.

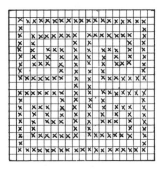

GREEK-KEY PILLOW
(inside back cover)

Color Key

☒	dark blue

This can be a striking design when stitched dark on white fabric or white on dark fabric.

UPHOLSTERY

Upholstering your miniature furniture will demonstrate your crafting abilities and your attention to detail—whether you build the furniture yourself or make it from the many kits available to miniature enthusiasts. Here are four different styles of traditional upholstery designs. The diagonal, zigzag and woven designs can be worked in needlepoint* or counted cross-stitch; the striped design can only be worked in counted cross-stitch. (If working the designs in needlepoint, use two strands of yarn for better coverage and texture.) The designs are continuous and can be repeated as often as necessary to bring the upholstery fabric to the correct size. The color keys given here are those I used for the pieces shown on the covers of this book; feel free to make up color schemes to coordinate with the furniture already in your dollhouse. These designs can be used to upholster sofas, chairs, benches, stools, even floor cushions.

If you are making furniture from a kit, patterns for the upholstery fabric will usually be included. Use these patterns to mark the outline of the pieces needed on Hardanger 22-per-inch counted-thread fabric or size 18 needlepoint canvas, keeping the grain straight and leaving ½″ between pieces. Mark the center of each fabric section to be worked with a pin;

embroider or needlepoint each piece following the chart you have selected and working outward from the center so the design is centered (where applicable). Finish the furniture following the instructions in the kit.

If you are building your own furniture, make your patterns with tissue paper from the actual pieces of furniture. Use the patterns to mark your fabric or canvas as described above. After the embroidery or needlepoint is complete, cut out the designs leaving ¼″ seam allowances around all edges that will be visible. Fold the seam allowances carefully to the wrong side. Apply clear acrylic spray to the wrong side to prevent glue from soaking through to the right side. Add a small amount of padding (cotton balls, polyester fiberfill) to the piece you are covering; keep this padding to a minimum to avoid the appearance of overstuffing. Brush undiluted glue onto the wood around the edges of the padding and attach the fabric or canvas, smoothing out any wrinkles or air bubbles and allowing the fabric or canvas to smoothly cover the padding. Try to position any raw edges where they will not be seen. To hide seams or raw edges, glue tiny cords or braided floss over glued edges.

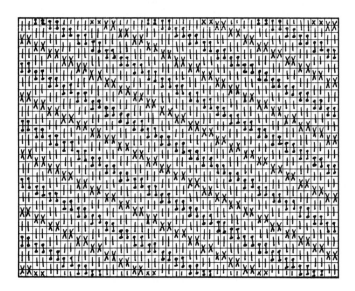

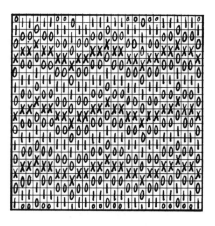

DIAGONAL

Color Key

❚ light green
❘ medium green
✕ dark green

ZIGZAG
(inside back cover)

Color Key

❘ light blue
0 medium blue
✕ dark blue

*For needlepoint, work in bargello stitch over number of mesh indicated on chart.

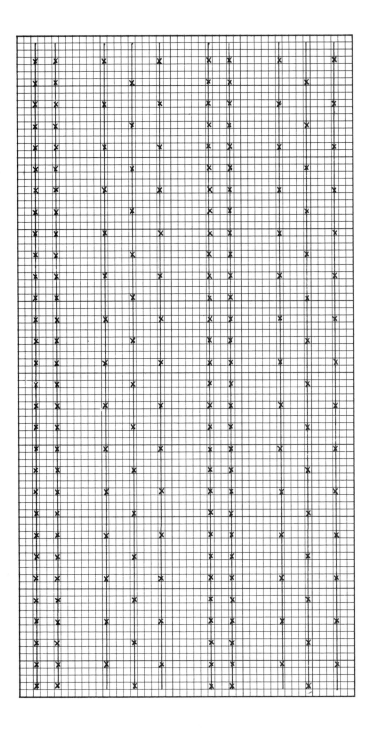

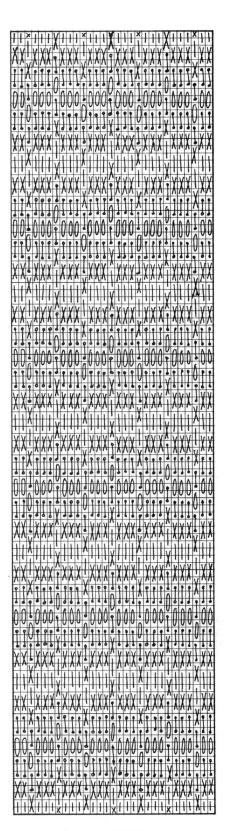

STRIPED
(inside back cover)

Color Key

X medium blue
| dark blue (laidwork)

Use six strands of dark blue for the laid-work; one strand of medium blue for the cross-stitches. Position the dark blue strand on the fabric; secure it in place by working medium blue cross-stitches over it.

WOVEN
(inside front cover)

Color Key

| pale pink   ▮ medium pink
X light pink   0 dark pink

CHAIR CUSHIONS

A great way to personalize purchased chairs is by adding a counted cross-stitch or needlepoint chair cushion. Measure the size of the area you wish to cover; the canvas or fabric should be ¼″ larger than that. Mark this measurement on your canvas or fabric, then work the design in the exact center of that area. The center of each of these designs is indicated with an arrow. Needlepoint designs will have less background area than the same designs done in counted cross-stitch. Chair cushions should be assembled in the same way as pillows; follow the general instructions on page 18, except use less stuffing. Ties may be added to the two back corners of the cushion; use three strands of embroidery floss in a matching color.

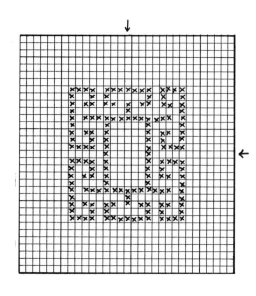

ORIENTAL CHAIR CUSHION
(front cover)

Color Key

☒   medium blue

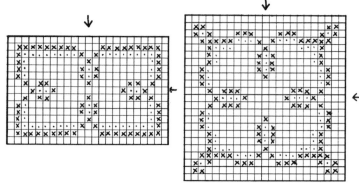

ROCKING-CHAIR HEAD AND SEAT CUSHIONS
(back cover)

Color Key

⊡   yellow   ☒   green

Attach yellow ties to adjacent corners along one long edge of the head cushion and to adjacent corners of the seat cushion.

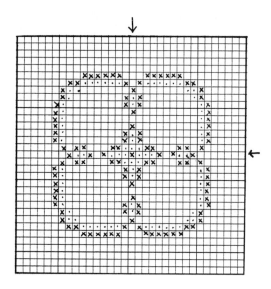

STYLIZED FLORAL SEAT CUSHION

Color Key

⊡   light pink   ☒   dark pink

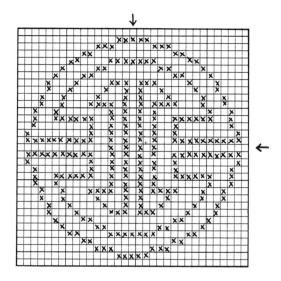

MEDALLION CHAIR CUSHION
(front cover)

Color Key

☒   blue

QUILTS

Probably no other single decorating element can add as much warmth and distinction to a room as a quilt. Here are three quilt patterns that can be worked in counted cross-stitch to add a touch of folk art and craftsmanship to a very special room. Substitute your own colors for the ones I have given so the quilts will perfectly match the rooms in which they'll reside.

Each quilt chart represents one quarter of the design—the lower right quarter. The instructions following each color key give the total dimensions of each finished quilt; allow an extra margin of fabric all around. Find the center of your fabric and mark it with a pin. Begin working the design from the center (indicated on the chart by a star); complete the chart as shown. Work the lower left quarter of the quilt by following the chart in reverse; do not repeat the center row indicated by an arrow at the bottom of the chart. Work the lower half of the quilt in reverse for the upper half.

Before cutting away the excess fabric, "paint" the wrong side of the outer border of the design and a few threads beyond it with diluted white glue; allow to dry thoroughly. Using sharp embroidery scissors, carefully cut the fabric one row of threads away from the embroidered border. For scalloped edges, simply follow the embroidery as a cutting guide, carefully clipping away the excess fabric at the indentations, forming the scallop so there is a one-thread border of fabric all around the quilt.

HOLE-IN-THE-BARN-DOOR QUILT
(inside front cover)

Color Key

⊡	light green
⊠	dark green

The dimensions of the finished quilt are 119 × 140; the background fabric should be ivory or white.

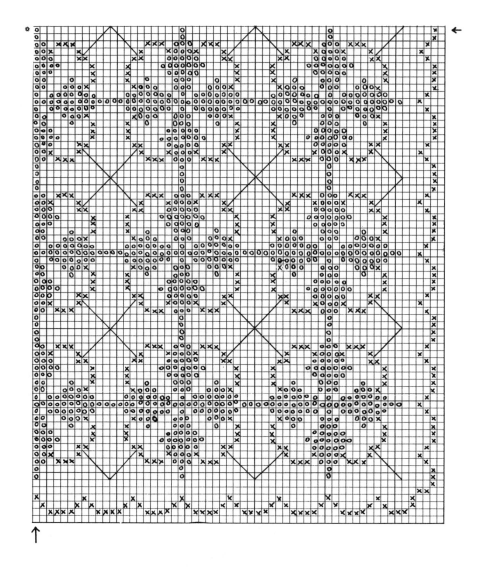

FOUR-WINDS QUILT
(inside back cover)

Color Key

☒ yellow
⌧ royal blue

The dimensions of the finished quilt are
117 × 138; the background fabric
should be a shade lighter than the
darkest color being used. Backstitch all
straight lines with one strand of royal
blue.

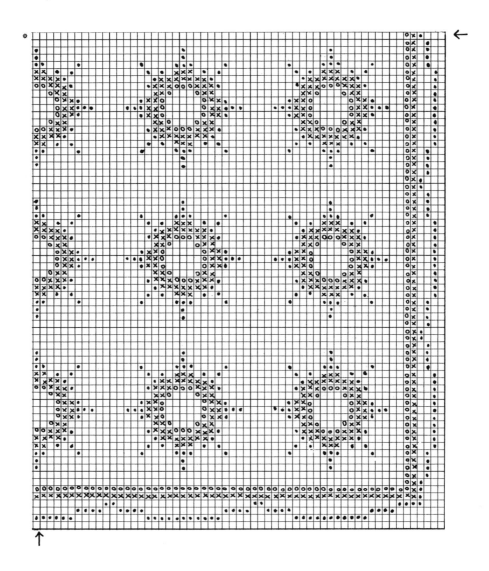

PRIMROSE QUILT

Color Key

☑ O	light yellow
☒ X	dark yellow
�」●	pale green

The dimensions of the finished quilt are 117 × 138; the background fabric should be ivory or white. Scallop the edges.

DECORATIVE ACCENT PIECES

Very often, accessories are what make a house a home—and miniature dollhouses are no exception! Included here is a variety of designs that will enhance already-decorated rooms or serve as a focal point for rooms that are about to be furnished.

Most of these designs will look best if worked in counted cross-stitch. After the embroidery is complete, finish the edges of the piece as follows: Decide upon the finished size of the piece; this will depend upon the size frame in which the piece will be fitted. The border of unworked fabric around each design can easily be adjusted to fit any existing frame. If you are framing the piece yourself, follow the outline I have indicated (the dark outline around the chart) for the best results. Then "paint" the wrong side of the design along the edge that will be cut with diluted white glue; allow to dry thoroughly. Using sharp embroidery scissors, carefully cut away the excess fabric.

Frame the piece with basswood stripping or a purchased frame by carefully gluing the wood to the fabric (mirror frame, samplers); cover the back of the piece with plain paper. If you are gluing the fabric to wood (fire screen, folding screens) use spray adhesive or diluted white glue, carefully smoothing away any wrinkles or air bubbles. Sew or glue hardware in place (bellpulls); do not trim edges until size has been determined by hardware.

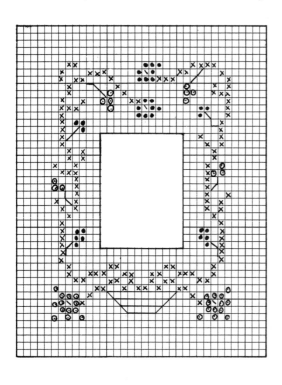

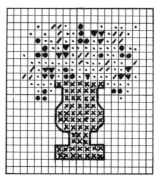

FLORAL MIRROR FRAME
(inside back cover)

Color Key

◙	dark yellow	◸	blue
◉	rose	⊠	green

Backstitch stems with one strand of green and basket with one strand of tan. After design has been embroidered, "paint" the inner edge of the frame with diluted white glue same as outer edge. Carefully cut out center section leaving two rows of unworked fabric as a border. Tape small rectangular mirror behind embroidered frame. Glue outer wooden frame in place, then cover entire back with plain white paper.

FIREPLACE SCREEN
(inside back cover)

Color Key

⊠	ivory	◫	orange
◉	yellow	⊡	green
▼	pink		

Backstitch outline of vase with one strand of tan. Cut fabric to fit fireplace screen and attach as directed. Design can also be framed and hung as a picture.

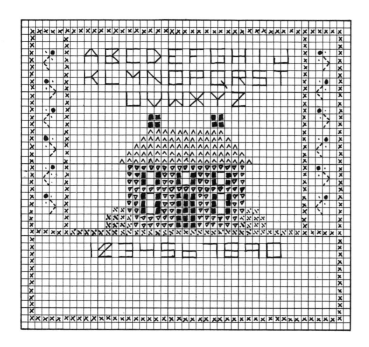

ALPHABET SAMPLER
(inside front cover)

Color Key

⊡	light pink	⊠	dark blue
⊙	rose	◩	dark green
⊽	red	▣	black
⋀	gray		

Your name and the date should be embroidered below the numerals; figure out the spacing by using the letters and numerals on the sampler. Use one strand of floss to work the following in backstitch: alphabet and numerals with medium blue, name and date below numerals with rose, window frames with black, stems (▨ ◪) with light green. Frame finished embroidery.

ARCH SAMPLER
(inside back cover)

Color Key

⊽	yellow	⊠	navy blue
⋀	gold	◭	gray
⊡	light rose	▨	brown
⊙	medium rose	▣	black
◸	green		

Your name should be embroidered in the space provided beneath the grass; figure out the spacing by using the letters on the sampler. Use one strand of floss to work the following in backstitch: alphabet and name with medium rose, girl's hair with yellow, boy's hair with black, columns with gold. Frame finished embroidery.

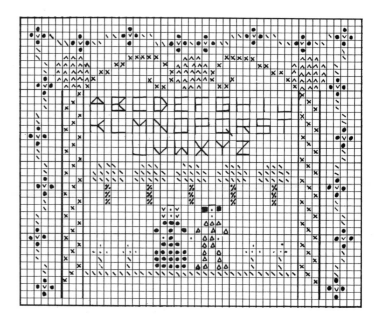

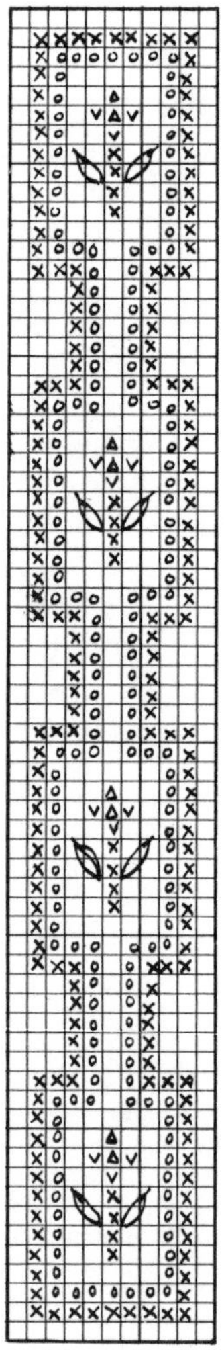

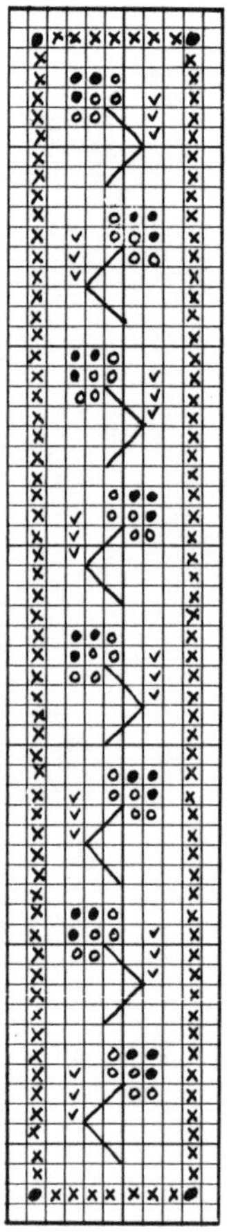

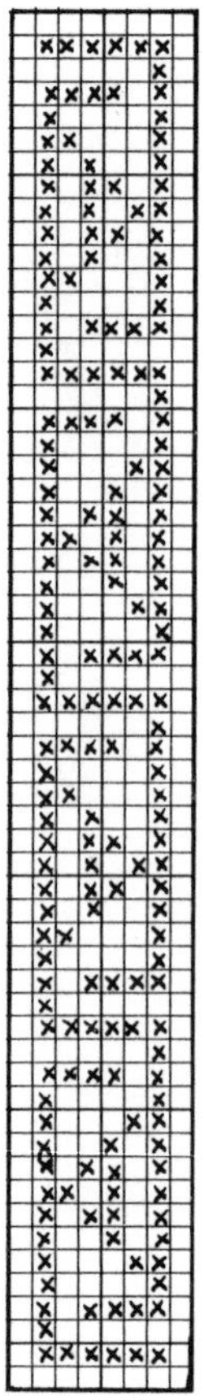

CASTELLATED BELLPULL

Color Key

- ☒V dark yellow
- ☒Δ medium blue
- ☒O medium green
- ☒X dark green
- dark green lazy daisy stitch (one strand)

FLORAL BELLPULL

(inside front cover)

Color Key

- O light pink
- ● rose
- V medium green
- X dark green

Backstitch stems with one strand of medium green.

GEOMETRIC BELLPULL

(front cover)

Color Key

- X ivory

Work this design on colored fabric.

FLORAL FOLDING SCREEN ▶

Color Key

- · yellow
- ● dark yellow
- Δ medium blue
- V medium green
- X brown

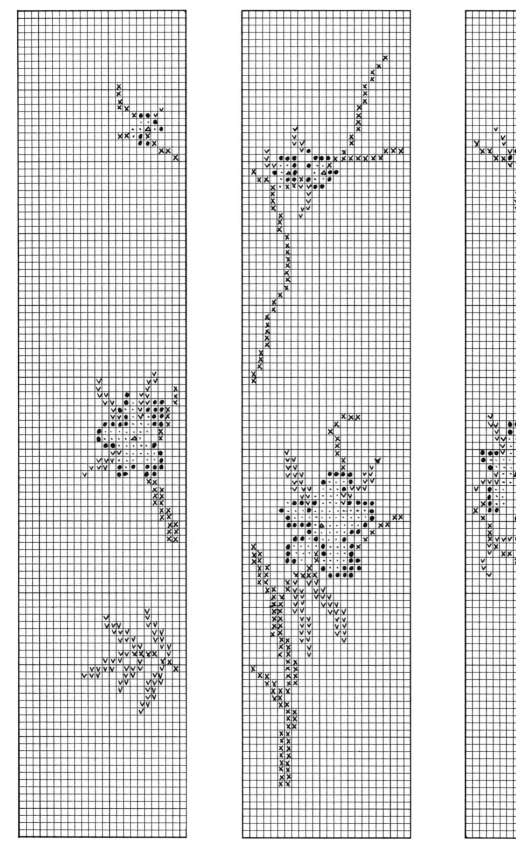

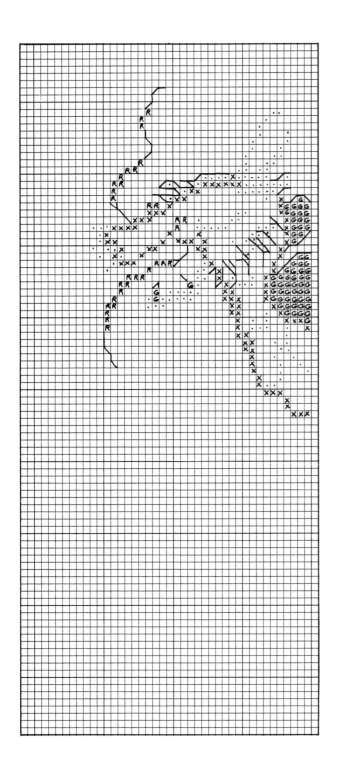
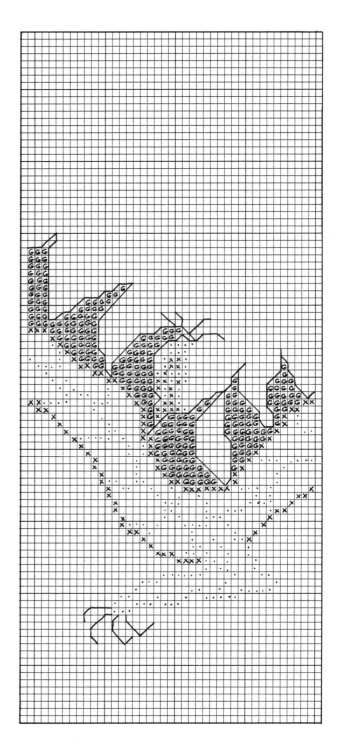

DRAGON FOLDING SCREEN
(front cover)

Color Key

R	red
G	light gray
·	medium blue
X	medium green

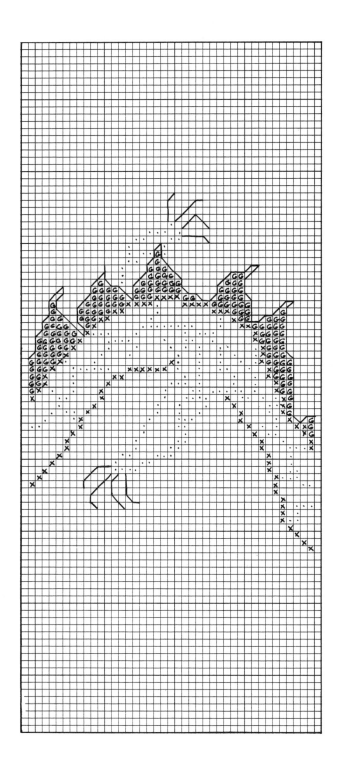

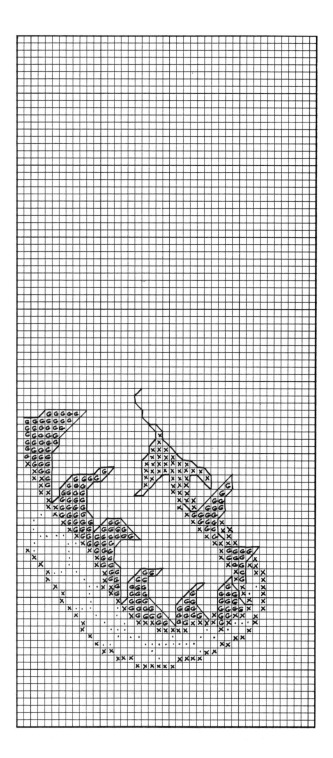

Fill in the body with medium green cross-stitches; these symbols were not drawn in, so that the chart would be easier to read. Use one strand of floss to work the following in backstitch after all cross-stitches are completed: flame with red, spikes around head and along back with dark blue, claws with black. This design would make a magnificent, large painting for a miniature Oriental room if embroidered in one piece; frame with basswood stripping. The design could quite easily be rendered in needlepoint for a full-scale wall hanging or pillow.

PLACE MATS AND NAPKINS

No dining room is complete without a matching set of place mats and napkins to coordinate with the decor of the room. I've designed six different sets that will fit into many decorating styles. These take no time at all to make and will add so much to your dining-room table. Work all the designs in counted cross-stitch on Hardanger 22-per-inch counted-thread fabric using one strand of floss. There are two ways to finish the edges after the embroidery is complete. For a straight edge, "paint" with diluted white glue, allow the glue to dry thoroughly, then cut out using sharp embroidery scissors. For a fringed edge, cut out three threads beyond the edge of the design, then draw out two threads all around.

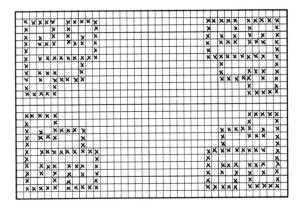

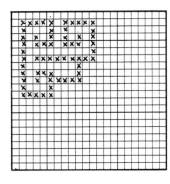

GEOMETRIC

Color Key

⊠ medium blue

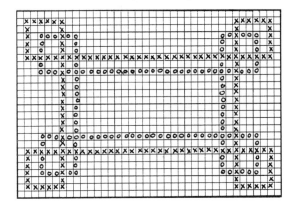

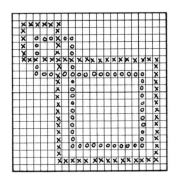

ECHOES

Color Key

⊙ medium blue
⊠ dark blue

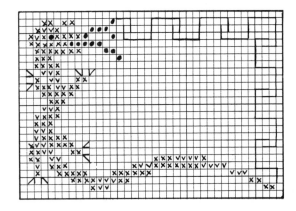

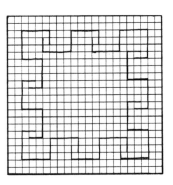

DRAGON
(front cover)

Color Key

⊙ red
Ⅴ medium blue
⊠ medium green

Backstitch claws and border with one strand of black.

MEDALLION

Color Key

☒ medium blue

Backstitch border
with one strand of
medium blue.

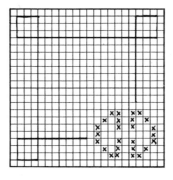

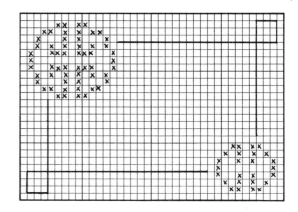

FLORAL
(front cover)

Color Key

⊡ yellow
☒ pink
◩ dark pink
⬤ green

Backstitch border
with one strand of
dark green.

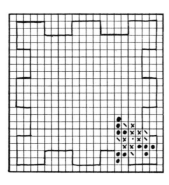

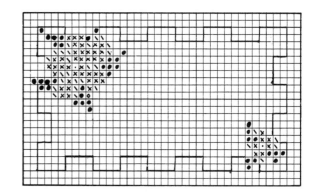

BOXES

Color Key

◘ medium blue
☒ dark blue

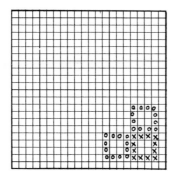

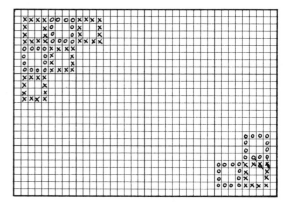

WINDOW TREATMENTS

Windows are significant elements in creating the illusion of realism in a dollhouse and it is important not to ignore them. On these two pages I have worked with one basic design, developing it in a variety of ways to embellish any number of windows. These designs should be worked in counted cross-stitch on Hardanger 22-per-inch counted-thread fabric using one strand of floss. The curtains may be lined with very lightweight fabric if they are going to be seen through a window. The curtains may also be used for bed hangings if you are decorating a canopy bed (see page 41); in this case the hangings must be lined.

The length of the curtains depends on the height of the window—determine the finished length of the curtains, then add ½″ for the curtain-rod casing if the curtains are not being lined. If you are lining the curtains, add ¼″ around all edges for the seam allowance. Work the curtain designs using colors to match your room; also make matching tiebacks and a valance if desired.

The cross-stitch design should extend to the top of the curtain. If curtains are not being lined, "paint" the wrong side of the design along the outer border and a few threads beyond it with diluted white glue, allow to dry thoroughly, then carefully cut away excess fabric using sharp embroidery scissors. If lining the curtains, sew lightweight fabric to curtain with right sides facing and raw edges even, making ¼″ seams; leave an opening at the bottom for turning and a ⅜″ opening at the top on each side for the casing. Turn to right side, folding raw edges at bottom and side openings inside; press carefully. Slip-stitch bottom opening closed. Topstitch curtain to lining ⅛″ and ⅜″ below top edge to form the casing.

Finish the tiebacks and valance by "painting" the edges with glue same as unlined curtains. The edges of the valance should be cut to follow the castellated border.

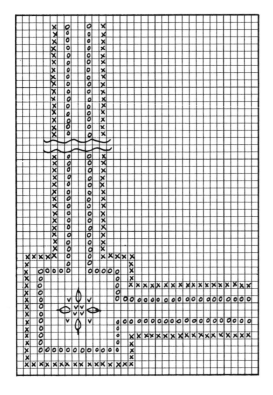

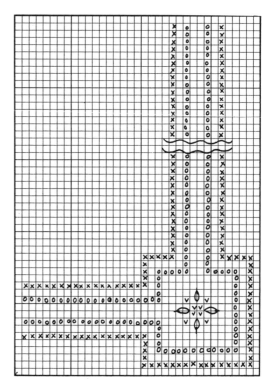

FLORAL CURTAINS (OR BED HANGINGS)

Color Key

V	yellow
O	medium green
X	dark green
◊	dark green lazy daisy stitch (one strand)

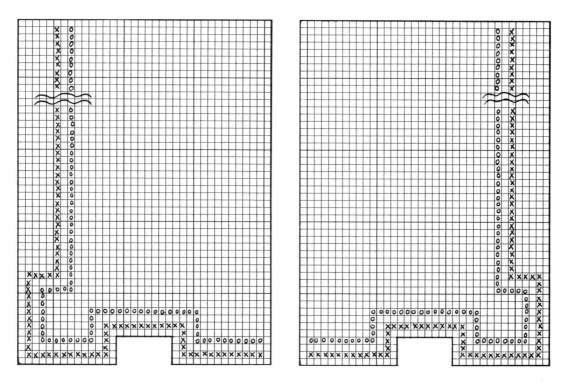

GEOMETRIC CURTAINS (OR BED HANGINGS)

Color Key

- ⊻ yellow
- ⊙ medium green
- ⊠ dark green
- ◊ dark green lazy daisy stitch (one strand)

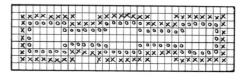

TIEBACK FOR CURTAINS

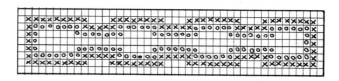

TIEBACK FOR BED HANGINGS

VALANCE

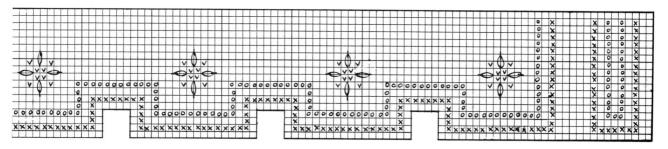

BEDSPREADS

Hand-embroidered bedspreads are a sure way to attract attention to your miniature bedrooms. Here are two bedspread designs from which to choose: the first is quite versatile and the second frankly feminine! These spreads will fit a standard 5″ × 6″ miniature bed with a 1″ overhang on three sides. For a bed with no footboard or posters, work the entire design, ignoring the square cutting lines in the corners. For a poster bed, eliminate the corners at the foot of the spread (indicated on the charts by the double lines). The inner line at the corner is the hemline; do not embroider any stitches beyond this line.

Work the designs in counted cross-stitch on Hardanger 22-per-inch counted-thread fabric using two strands of floss. The charts are half-patterns; work the first half in reverse for the second half.

After the embroidery is complete and before cutting away the excess fabric, "paint" the wrong side of the outer border of the design and a few threads beyond it with diluted white glue; allow to dry thoroughly. Using sharp embroidery scissors, carefully cut the fabric one row of threads away from the embroidered border. For scalloped or castellated edges, simply follow the embroidery as a cutting guide, carefully clipping away the excess fabric so there is a one-thread border of fabric all around the bedspread. To hem the corners of a bedspread for a poster bed, clip along the diagonal line shown on chart, fold the hem to the wrong side and glue in place.

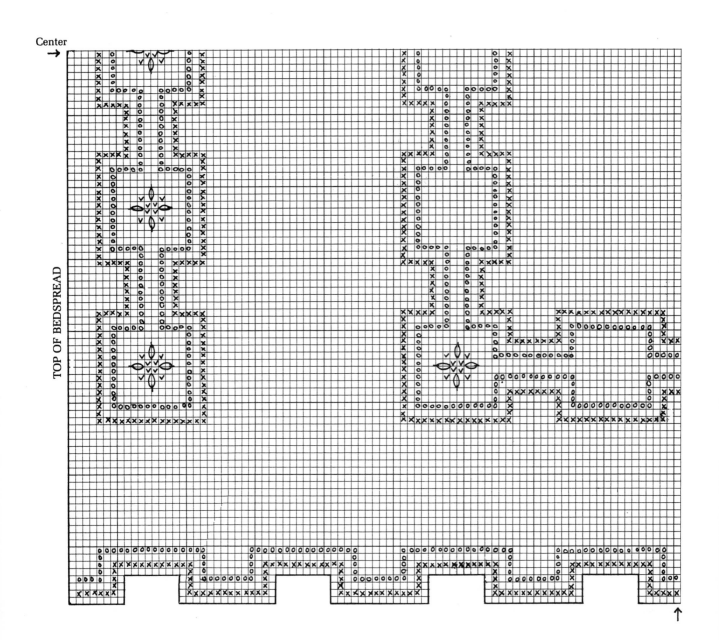

Center →

TOP OF BEDSPREAD

CASTELLATED BEDSPREAD

Color Key

V yellow
O medium green
X dark green
    dark green lazy daisy stitch
    (one strand)

Cut the edges of the bedspread to follow the castellated border. This spread and its matching canopy (see pages 40–41) were designed to coordinate with the window treatments on pages 34–35.

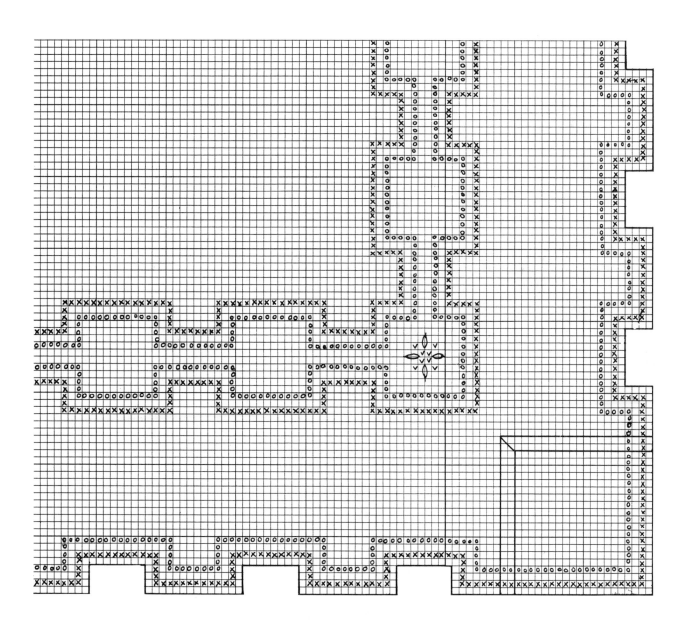

TOP OF BEDSPREAD

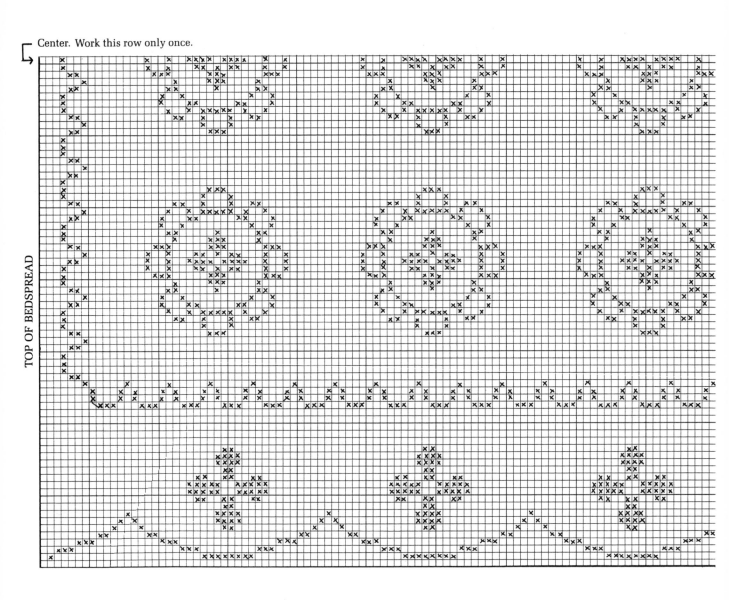

FLORAL BEDSPREAD
(inside front cover)

Color Key

⊠ pink

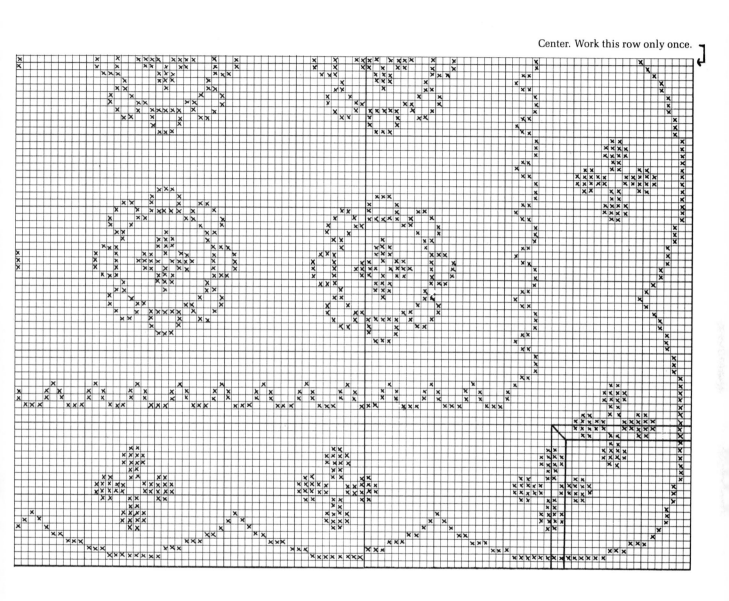

This design can be made to look like a
Martha Washington bedspread if French
knots are worked in white on a white
fabric or in ecru on an ecru fabric. For a
colorful bedspread for a child's room,
work the flowers in different primary
colors.

CANOPIES

A canopy bed is always elegant and very much admired. These designs will take no time at all to make because you are only embroidering a simple border on each! These canopies will fit a standard 5″ × 6″ miniature bed; to alter the size, increase or decrease the number of stitches at the bottom of each castellation or scallop.

Work the designs in counted cross-stitch on Hardanger 22-per-inch counted-thread fabric using two strands of floss. The charts are half-patterns; work the first half in reverse for the second half.

After the embroidery is complete and before cutting away the excess fabric, "paint" the wrong side of the outer border of the design and a few threads beyond it with diluted white glue; allow to dry thoroughly.

Using sharp embroidery scissors, carefully cut the fabric one row of threads away from the embroidered border. For castellated or scalloped edges, simply follow the embroidery as a cutting guide, carefully clipping away the excess fabric so there is a one-thread border of fabric all around the canopy. All four corners of the canopy are hemmed (indicated on the charts by the double lines). To hem the corners, clip along the diagonal line shown on the chart, fold the hem to the wrong side and glue in place. Very light fabric may be used as a lining to hide the stitches; glue lining to canopy around the edges before cutting away excess fabric, allow to dry, then cut out as one unit. Hemming is not necessary if the canopy is lined.

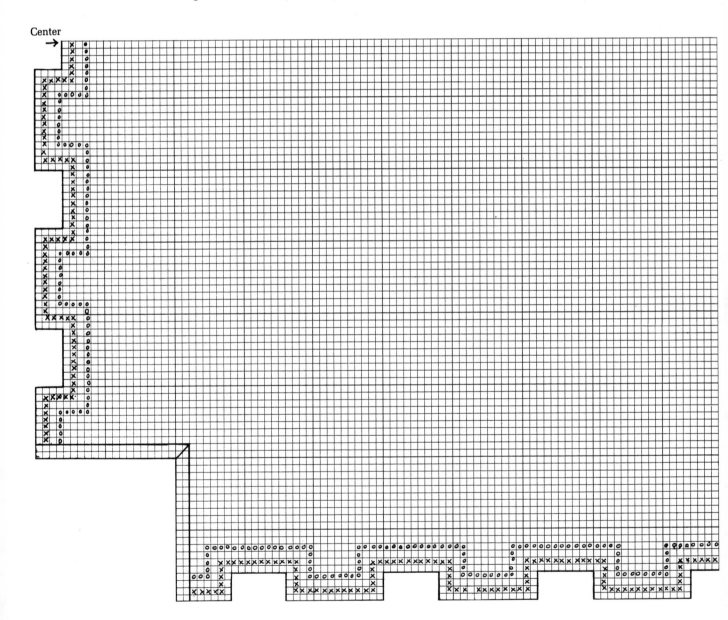

Center

CASTELLATED CANOPY

Color Key

☐ medium green
☒ dark green

This canopy and its matching bedspread (see pages 36–37) were designed to coordinate with the window treatments on pages 34–35. If you are making this for a formal canopy bed, you may want to add bed hangings, also found on pages 34–35. Measure the height of the canopy to determine the length needed, then follow the instructions for lining curtains to complete the bed hangings; omit the casing at the top.

Center ←

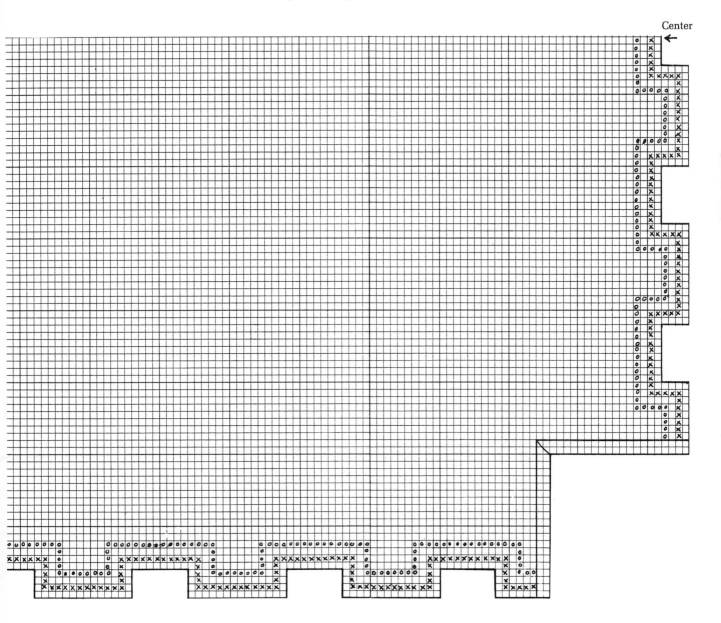

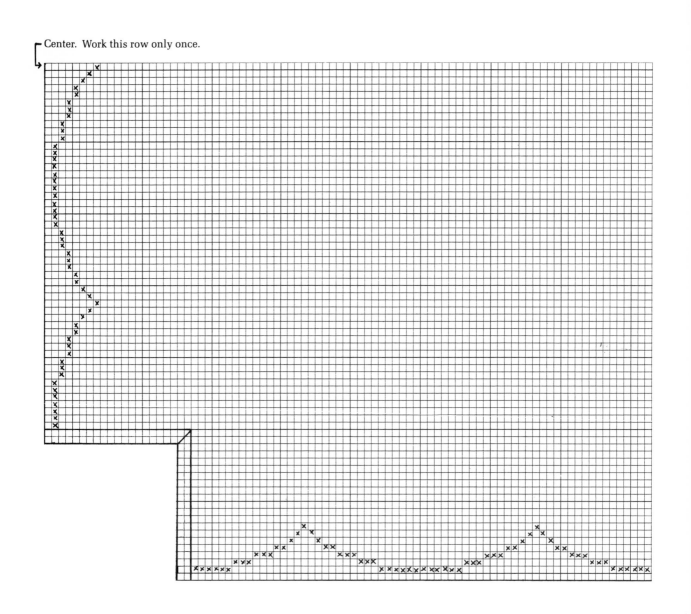

SCALLOPED CANOPY
(inside front cover)

Color Key

☒ pink

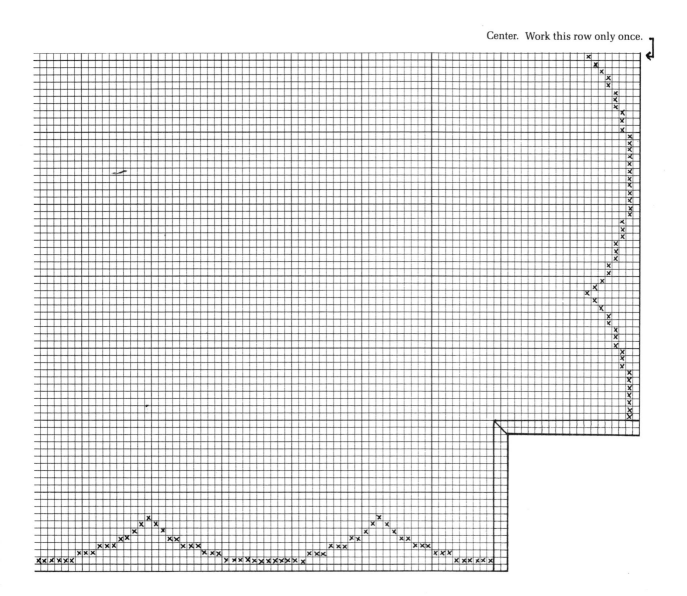

This canopy, while designed to coordinate with the Floral Bedspread (see pages 38–39), is simple and classic enough to match bedding you may already have. A spectacular way to dress up a tired old bed is to add a canopy!

NURSERY ACCESSORIES

If your dollhouse has an extra room and you are wondering what to do with it, why not consider making it into a nursery? Nurseries can be so much fun to decorate, and here are a few accessories to help you get started.

Most of these projects can be finished as directed in other sections of this book; page references for finishing instructions are given with each chart. Work all projects in counted cross-stitch on Hardanger 22-per-inch counted-thread fabric using one strand of floss unless otherwise directed.

BUNNY NURSERY ACCESSORIES

Color Key

- ◩ white (use two strands)
- ⊡ yellow
- ◮ orange
- ☒ dark green
- ▽ brown
- ⊙ dark brown

whiskers   dark brown

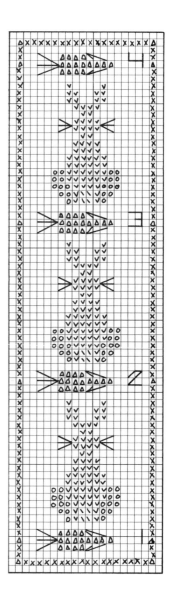

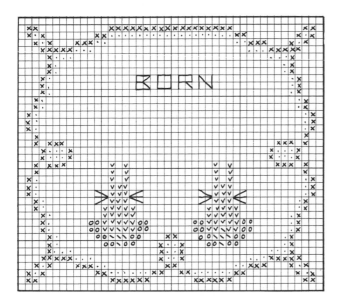

BIRTH SAMPLER
(back cover)

The baby's name, the date and place of birth should be embroidered beneath "Born"; figure out the spacing by using the letters and numerals on the Alphabet Sampler (page 27). Use one strand of floss to work the following in backstitch: "Born" with light green; name, date and place of birth with dark green. See page 26 for finishing instructions. Frame finished embroidery.

HEIGHT CHART
(back cover)

Use one strand of floss to work the following in backstitch: carrot tops and numerals with dark green, carrots with orange. See page 26 for finishing instructions. To hang height chart, use six strands of dark green embroidery floss, 2½" long. Knot the floss ¼" from each end to form tassels. Stitch knots to top corners of hanging so tassels extend outward at each side; floss in between will form hanging loop.

STUFFED BUNNY TOY
(back cover)

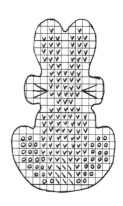

Make two pieces. Finish edges as directed on page 26, cutting out pieces two threads beyond edge of embroidery. Hold pieces together with wrong sides facing and backstitch to secure, adding small amount of stuffing before sewing opening closed.

BUNNY NURSERY ACCESSORIES

Color Key

- ◩   white (use two strands)
- ⊡   yellow
- ▲   orange
- ☒   dark green
- ⩔   brown
- ⊙   dark brown

whiskers   dark brown

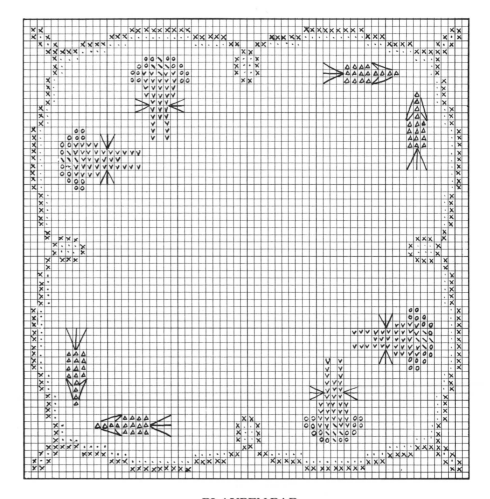

PLAYPEN PAD
(back cover)

Measure interior of playpen; add ½″ to measurements. Mark these measurements on counted-thread fabric, then work design in center. See page 22 for finishing instructions.

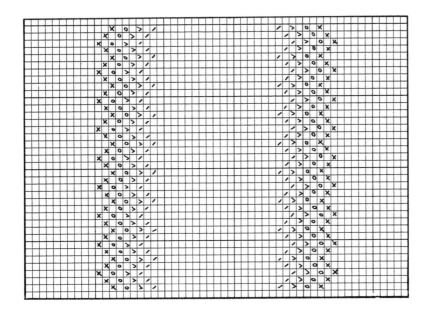

ZIGZAG RECEIVING BLANKET
(back cover)

Color Key

⧄	yellow
⊙	pink
⊠	blue
⊳	green

See page 23 for finishing instructions.

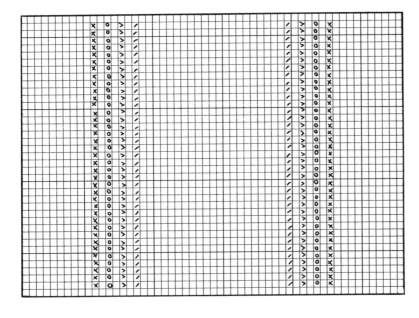

STRIPED RECEIVING BLANKET
(back cover)

Color Key

⧄	yellow
⊙	pink
⊠	blue
⊳	green

See page 23 for finishing instructions.

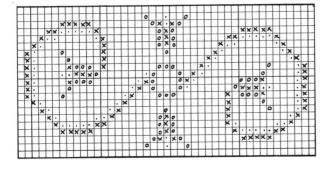

CRIB PILLOW
(back cover)

Color Key

·	light yellow
⊙	medium yellow
⊠	medium green

See page 18 for finishing instructions.

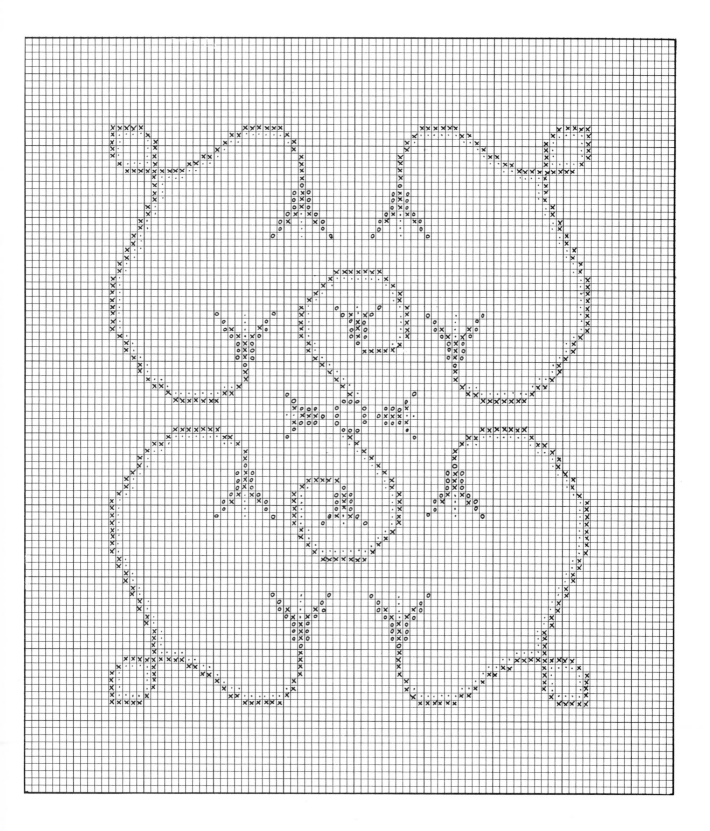

CRIB COVERLET
(back cover)

Color Key

⊡ light yellow
◙ medium yellow
⊠ medium green

After embroidery is complete, cut out coverlet along marked line (indicated by dark outline on chart). Make ½" fringe around edges of coverlet by drawing away 11 threads from each edge.